THE WOW AND THE HOW

SPACE

AMELIA MARSHALL

Gareth Stevens
PUBLISHING

Please visit our website, www.garethstevens.com. For a free color catalog of all our high-quality books, call toll free 1-800-542-2595 or fax 1-877-542-2596.

Cataloging-in-Publication Data
Names: Marshall, Amelia.
Title: Space / Amelia Marshall.
Description: Buffalo, NY : Gareth Stevens Publishing, 2026. | Series: The wow and the how | Includes glossary and index.
Identifiers: ISBN 9781482473155 (pbk.) | ISBN 9781482473162 (library bound) | ISBN 9781482473179 (ebook)
Subjects: LCSH: Outer space--Juvenile literature.
Classification: LCC QB500.22 M374 2026 | DDC 520--dc23

Published in 2026 by
Gareth Stevens Publishing
2544 Clinton St.
Buffalo, NY 14224

First published in Great Britain in 2024 by Hodder & Stoughton

Authors: Paul Rockett, Victoria Brooker, Amy Pimperton, Julia Bird, Grace Glendinning, Elise Short, Melanie Palmer

Series designer: Rocket Design (East Anglia) Ltd

Picture credits:
NASA: Bill Ingalls 27t; Johnson 26-27.
Shutterstock: Abudzar 8c; Ahmadalfant 10bl; AlexLMX 19c; Aphellon/elements furnished by NASA 6-7bg; Artsiom P/Elements furnished by NASA 28-29; Arvitalyaart front cover bg; ayelet-keshet 18b; BarboS 20-21bg; BlueRingMedia 4tr, 4cl, 5cr, 21b; BNP Design Studio 3b, 23b, 28c, 33b; Anna Bo 26, 30; Boyko Pictures 15b; BTC Studio 4-5; Catalyst Labs 6cl; Catmando/elements furnished by NASA 16-17; June Color 11b; Creative Shahin 10; Vasilii Duda 15cl, 15cr; Ezida112 5br, 9b; Markus Gann 12; Guingm 2, 25b; Iconic Bestiary 17c; Inspiring team 5r; klyaksun 2tl, 20tr; 20bl, 21c; Lineartestpilot 13cr, 14c, 13cr; Macrovector 8cb; K K T Madhusanka 29c; Keng Merry front cover l,1l; Zoran Milic 21tr; NASA Images 18-19; Georgio Nikaragua 22bl; Oixxo 5l, 29b; Olliven 24b; Jurick Peter 7b, 24-25; Pikovit 7c; Yulia R 13c; Larry-Rains 23c; Sabelskaya 32; Sensvector 22-23; Siridhata 6cr; Olexander Sirko 25c, 33t; Sweet Kiki 4tl; Tartila 19b, 27b; Tenstudio 3tr, 9c; Cory Thoman 17b; Dim Tik 5bl; 21studiodesign 8tr; VectorMine 13b; Yaroslav Vitkovskiy 8-9bg; Zakhachuck/elements furnished by NASA 14-15bg; Dima Zel front cover r, 1r.

All additional design elements from Shutterstock or drawn by designer.

Printed in the United States of America

CPSIA compliance information: Batch #CSGS26: For further information contact Gareth Stevens at 1-800-542-2595.

Find us on

CONTENTS

The WOW of space! → 4

In space, no one can hear you scream! → 6

Mars is as cold as the South Pole! → 8

Jupiter is bigger than all the other planets combined! → 10

Some stars can explode! → 12

The Milky Way eats other galaxies! → 14

Uranus is the only planet on its side! → 16

Venus' day is longer than its year! → 18

In space, liquid always forms a sphere! → 20

There's no wind on the moon! → 22

Falling into a black hole can make you into spaghetti! → 24

Astronauts actually GROW when they're in space! → 26

Some planets are just big balls of gas! → 28

Glossary → 30

Further reading → 31

Index → 32

THE WOW OF SPACE!

Space is AMAZING!
It stretches for millions of miles and is full of planets, asteroids and meteoroids.
WOW!

We know about **HOW** things move and exist in space because of space scientists, such as astronomers and astronauts. They study space and tell us all about it.

Discover amazing facts about space including some that may challenge what you thought you knew. Find out the science behind the facts to understand a bit more about it. Can you find your own **WOW** facts about space?

WOW!

In space, no one can hear you scream!

THESE TWO CAN SHOUT ALL THEY LIKE, IT'S NOT GOING TO HELP! **SOUND**–AS WE HEAR IT ON EARTH–DOESN'T EXIST IN SPACE.

HOW?

Here on Earth, you can hear sound because it travels as waves through matter such as air (gases), water (liquid), or walls (solid). Sound makes tiny bits of matter, also known as particles, vibrate. These vibrations are what we hear.

In space, on the other hand, there isn't much matter floating around. This means there aren't many particles to vibrate and create sound.

AMAZING SPACE

Scientists have detected waves rippling out of a black hole and managed to convert them into sounds that humans can hear. It is a very low rumble.

WOW!

Mars is as cold as the South Pole!

HOW?

The lowest ground temperature recorded on Earth is -128.6°F (-89.2°C) in Antarctica. Mars is about 56 million miles (90 million km) farther away from the sun than Earth. That means it gets a lot less light and heat to keep it warm. Mars also can't hold onto the heat it has.

On Earth, the sun's heat gets trapped in the atmosphere, which acts like a blanket to keep our planet warm. Mars' atmosphere is about a hundred times thinner than Earth's so any heat from the sun easily escapes.

AMAZING SPACE

On Mars, you can jump three times higher than on Earth. This is because Mars' gravity, the force that keeps us on the ground, is much weaker.

WOW!

Jupiter is bigger than all the other planets combined!

JUPITER IS SO BIG THAT ALL OF THE OTHER PLANETS IN THE SOLAR SYSTEM COULD FIT INSIDE IT!

HOW?

The early solar system was a vast, swirling cloud of gases and dust that were constantly bumping into each other. Gravity helped most of this matter clump together slowly over time to become our star, the sun. Like the sun, Jupiter is mostly made up of hydrogen and helium gases and it formed in the same way.

Jupiter's huge gravity slings comets out of the solar system, protecting Earth from them.

AMAZING SPACE

Jupiter is big, but it is dwarfed by the sun. The sun could fit about 1,000 Jupiters in it!

WOW!

Some stars can explode!

WHEN BIG STARS EXPLODE IT'S ONE OF THE MOST VIOLENT EVENTS IN THE UNIVERSE!

HOW?

A star uses fuel, such as hydrogen gas, to make heat and light. All the heat energy flowing outwards creates pressure. The force of this pressure resists the huge gravitational pull of the star's core to stop it collapsing in on itself.

A few billion or million years later, the star's fuel runs out. This upsets the forces keeping the star stable because the star can't create any new heat and pressure. Gravity takes over and the star's iron core collapses. Seconds later, the shockwave created by the core's collapse makes the outer layers of the star explode in a supernova. This massive boom flings the star's outer layers far into space.

AMAZING SPACE

A supernova star then becomes either a black hole or a neutron star. Neutron stars are so dense that a spoonful of one weighs as much as Mount Everest!

WOW!

The Milky Way eats other galaxies!

THE MILKY WAY IS MADE UP OF AT LEAST **100 BILLION STARS** AND IS HOME TO OUR PLANET EARTH. IT IS ONE OF MANY GALAXIES IN THE UNIVERSE.

HOW?

Ten billion years ago, the Milky Way collided with one of its neighboring galaxies, Gaia-Enceladus, eating it up! Galaxy collisions are common in the universe.

Galaxies are made up of stars, gas, rocks, and dust. The gravity of a large galaxy will pull a smaller one towards it. The larger galaxy begins to change the smaller one and merge into it. Scientists like to imagine the "collision" as two swarms of bees flying towards each other and becoming one big swarm.

AMAZING SPACE

The Milky Way will eventually be eaten by another galaxy, Andromeda. Don't worry though. This won't take place for at least another 4 billion years!

WOW! Uranus is the only planet on its side!

MOST OF THE PLANETS IN THE SOLAR SYSTEM SPIN COUNTER-CLOCKWISE, BUT URANUS TURNS CLOCKWISE! EVEN MORE UNUSUALLY, URANUS ROTATES ON ITS SIDE!

HOW?

Scientists think that Uranus' odd orbit was caused by a collision with another huge object in space. This odd tilt makes Uranus appear to spin sideways. Because of Uranus' tilt, the sun shines directly over each pole for nearly a quarter of the year. This plunges the other half of the planet into a 21-Earth-year winter! Brr!

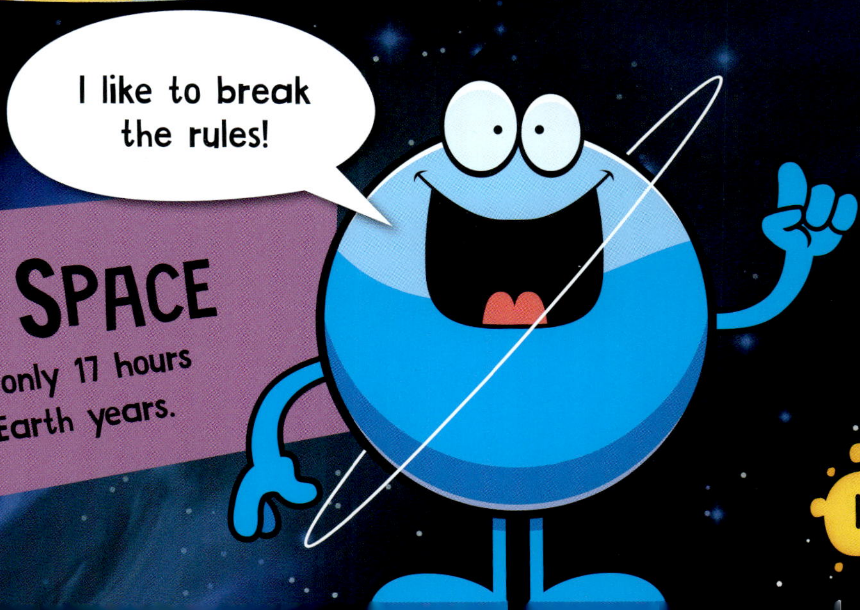

AMAZING SPACE

A day on Uranus is only 17 hours and a year is 84 Earth years.

WOW!

Venus' day is longer than its year!

ON VENUS, YOU WOULD TURN **ONE YEAR** OLD BEFORE YOU TURNED **ONE DAY** OLD.

HOW?

All the planets of our solar system travel around the sun on their own path, or orbit, and they all rotate on an axis.

ONE ORBIT AROUND THE SUN = the planet's year (on Earth this takes about 365 days)
ONE ROTATION ON ITS AXIS = the planet's day (on Earth this takes about 24 hours)

Venus is unique in our solar system because it orbits faster than it rotates. Venus takes about 243 Earth days to rotate once on its axis. It only takes 225 Earth days to orbit the sun.

Venus orbits so much quicker than Earth because it's close to the sun. Some scientists think it rotates slowly on its axis because it's spinning in the opposite direction to the rest of the planets. Venus is all mixed up!

AMAZING SPACE

Look up! Venus is the second brightest object in the sky after the moon. You can sometimes even see it in the daytime if you know where to look.

WOW!

In space, liquid always forms a sphere!

IN SPACE, WHERE EVERYTHING IS IN FREE FALL, LIQUID GATHERS IN SPHERES.

Floating is such fun!

HOW?

On Earth, gravity forces any liquid downwards, so it takes the shape of its container–whether that's an ocean or a drinking glass!

Without gravity in space, the molecules join together. Each molecule pulls on neighboring molecules with equal tension creating surface tension. Surface tension is the force at the top of a liquid that forms an upper layer like skin. This tension always creates a shape with the smallest surface area, which in space is a sphere.

AMAZING SPACE

Water exists all over the solar system, usually as ice. It's found in most comets and asteroids and on many planets too.

WOW!

There's no wind on the moon!

IN FACT, YOU DON'T REALLY EXPERIENCE ANY KIND OF WEATHER ON THE MOON.

HOW?

The moon doesn't have an atmosphere, at least not a dense one like Earth's, just a very thin exosphere, or outer layer. Weather is essentially due to the atmosphere. That's why you won't feel wind or see clouds or rainfall on the moon.

You do get "space weather" on the moon though. Solar winds (charged particles from the sun) or meteoroid streams (dust from comets) can affect the moon's surface.

AMAZING SPACE

The temperature on the moon varies from super hot to super cold! It can reach a scorching 250°F (121°C) in the sun's rays, but without them, the temperature can plummet to -208°F (-133°C)!

WOW!

Falling into a black hole can make you into spaghetti!

HOW?

Black holes are similar to magnets in that they attract everything around them. Black holes have such a strong gravitational pull that they pull everything nearby into it. If you were unfortunate enough to fall out of your spacecraft and be dragged towards a black hole, it wouldn't be long before you were "spaghettified!"

Spaghettification describes what happens when something falls into a black hole. Any object falling towards a black hole will be stretched and pulled into long thin shapes, just like pieces of spaghetti!

AMAZING SPACE

The first black hole was identified in the early 1970s, but we still aren't quite sure how they work.

WOW!

Astronauts actually GROW when they're in space!

ASTRONAUTS CAN GROW A FEW CENTIMETERS TALLER.

HOW?

It's all down to gravity—or more accurately, microgravity. Microgravity means when gravity is not very strong. Astronauts on longer space missions float around in microgravity for months at a time. While they're bouncing around on the ceiling, their bodies are free from the pressure of the gravity we experience back here on Earth. As a result, their spines stretch out a little, making them grow taller!

U.S. astronaut Kate Rubins grew 1 inch (3 cm) during her trip to space!

It's only temporary though. When astronauts return to Earth, gravity takes over again, and they gradually shrink back to their original height. At least they don't need to buy new clothes.

AMAZING SPACE

You experience a similar thing every night in bed. While you sleep, your spine stretches and gets longer. You can grow up to 0.4 inch (1 cm) by the morning!

WOW!

Some planets are just big balls of gas!

PLANETS CAN BE MOSTLY MADE UP OF GAS, SO THERE'S NO WAY YOU CAN WALK ON THEM.

How?

The four planets most distant from the sun—Jupiter, Saturn, Uranus, and Neptune—are known as the gas giants. They are much bigger than Earth and are essentially giant balls of gas, just like stars. These planets have no solid surface. The gas circles around a small metallic or rocky center. It is held in place by forces.

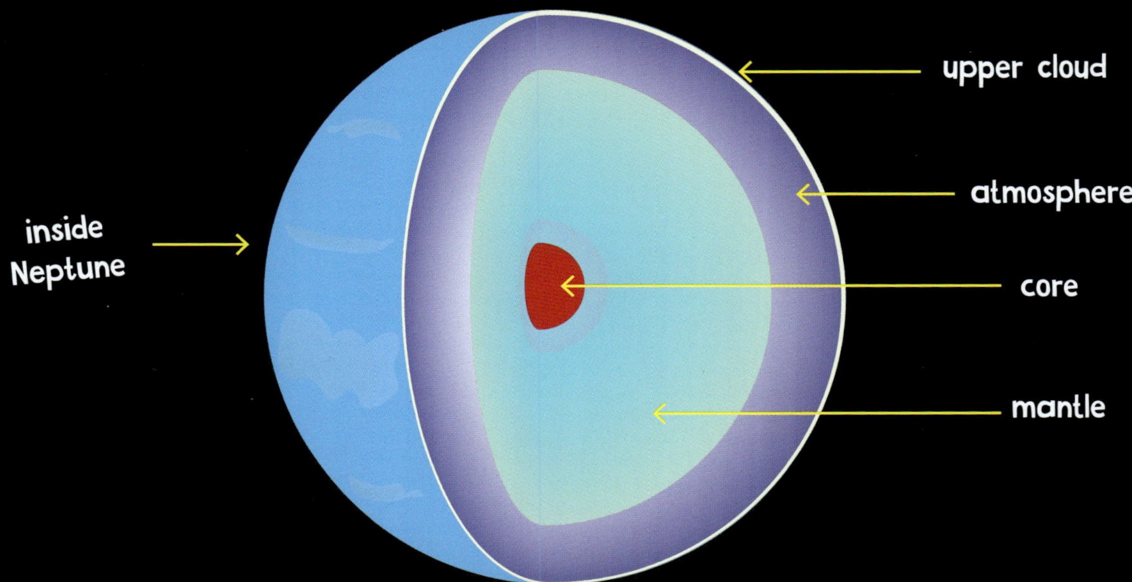

Amazing Space

Each of the gas giants also has a ring system. These rings are made up of ice, dust, and small rocks.

GLOSSARY

asteroid a large rocky object which orbits the sun

atmosphere the layer of gases surrounding Earth or another planet

axis an imaginary line through an object, around which it turns (rotates)

black hole an area in space which pulls everything into it, even light

comet an object made of ice, dust, and bits of rock, with a long fiery "tail" that travels through space in a long orbit around the sun

core central part of something

galaxy a huge collection of stars and their solar systems

gravity the pulling force between all objects. On Earth, it pulls us towards the ground.

meteoroid a rocky object which orbits the sun and is smaller than an asteroid

molecule a group of one or more atoms held together to form a substance

neutron star the collapsed remains of a giant star

solar system the sun and everything that moves around it (planets, comets etc)

vibration a shaking movement

FURTHER READING

BOOKS

Comic Strip Science: Earth and Space
by Paul Mason (Wayland, 2022)

So Many Questions about Space
by Sally Spray and Mark Ruffle (Wayland, 2022)

Space
by Meg Marquardt (Early Encyclopedias, 2025)

WEBSITES

www.bbc.co.uk/bitesize/topics/zkbbkqt
Here is lots of information about space.

www.nasa.gov/kidsclub/index.html
Find out all about space and play some games with NASA's own Kids' Club.

www.natgeokids.com/uk/discover/science/space/ten-facts-about-space/
More amazing facts about space.

INDEX

asteroids 4, 11, 21
astronauts 5, 26–27

black holes 7, 13, 24–25

comets 11, 21, 23

galaxies 14–15
gas giants 28–29
gravity 9, 11, 13, 21, 25, 27

Jupiter 10–11, 29

Mars 8–9
meteoroids 4, 23
Milky Way 14–15
molecules 21
moon 19, 22–23

Neptune 29

Saturn 29
solar system 10–11, 16, 19, 21
sound (in space) 6–7
stars 11–15, 29 *see also* sun
  neutron stars 13
  supernovas 13
sun 9, 11, 17, 19, 23, 29

universe 12, 14–15
Uranus 16–17, 29

Venus 18–19